Money is an Idea:

Effective Techniques for Acquiring Skills

I0465431

By

Gyabaah Gilbert Yeboah

Table of Contents

Introduction

The Seed of Prosperity.

Consider standing in a big orchard full of healthy, bountiful trees. Consider someone offering you a single seed and stating, "This is all you need to grow your own." At first, it may seem too little and unimportant to produce anything useful. But here's the secret: that seed is an idea with endless potential—if nurtured.

Like trees, money doesn't just appear; it's the result of carefully planted, nurtured, and produced ideas. Each dollar you make depends on your ability to value an idea. And every skill you learn is a tool for making that change more efficient and effective.

This book will teach you how to master the art of sowing seeds— turning ideas into opportunities and then into money. You'll see how learning skills is more than simply a method of survival; it's a dynamic plan for living the life you want.

So let's go into the orchard together. With the proper skills and a little patience, you'll soon be harvesting the abundance you've always desired. After all, money is a concept rather than a physical object. And your next big idea may be the one that transforms everything.

The Power of an Idea.

Close your eyes and imagine yourself standing at the edge of a bustling market. People are constantly exchanging goods, making deals, and generating wealth. You pay close attention and notice something fascinating: every success story in that market starts with one simple idea.

Now imagine this. You hold a blank sheet of paper, your mind racing with ideas. That paper represents possibility, but without action, it is empty. The key to transforming that blank space into a masterpiece of success is what you know and are willing to learn.

More than paper and numbers, money is ideas in motion. Every skill you learn is a new tool, and each tool improves your ability to turn ideas into successful realities. Whether you want to master a skill, start a business, or simply improve your life, the techniques in this book are your guide.

In Money is an Idea: Effective Techniques for Acquiring Skills, we'll look at how the right mindset and skill set can propel you from dream to action. You'll learn how to realize your full potential, develop valuable skills, and convert those skills into streams of opportunity.

Chapter 1: Foundation of Skill Mastery.

In today's environment, financial success is defined by the purposeful and continuous development of relevant talents instead of fate or connections. Whether you're an entrepreneur, employee, or freelancer, your ability to learn, improve, and use the correct talents will determine the course of your financial destiny. Skill mastery is the foundation of success in every industry, and it has never been more accessible to those who are ready to put in the work.

Exploring the Role of Skills in Financial Success.

The mastery of skills is essential to any adept profession and business. Financial success is directly related to how effectively you can exploit your skills in the marketplace. Think about the most successful individuals you know, whether they are top executives, successful company owners, or high-performing freelancers. What makes them apart? They can not only master a given skill set but also develop and adapt to changing circumstances.

The contemporary economy operates based on skills. They decide your market worth, affect your career prospects, and have a direct effect on your earnings potential. The beauty of talents is that they are transportable and can be employed across a broad range of sectors. For example, a person with strong communication skills may flourish as a leader, marketer, or salesman. A smart programmer may go from developing applications to founding a technology firm. The secret to financial success, therefore, is not to depend on external forces such as chance or fate, but to constantly grow and refine your skills.

The Concept of Deliberate Practice.

Mastery does not happen by chance. It's the consequence of intentional practice, which is a systematic, goal-oriented procedure for gradually enhancing certain talents. The goal of deliberate practice is to push your limits and improve in specific areas. This is where most individuals fall short. They practice for hours without progress.

When you participate in purposeful practice, you are intentionally working outside of your comfort zone. You're attempting to overcome deficiencies, broaden your knowledge, and improve your skills. For example, if you're learning to play the guitar, just strumming along with tunes you already know won't suffice. To develop, work on difficult chords, practice finger skills, and push yourself with new and complicated works.

The same idea applies to every ability that you want to perfect. For example, if you're an aspiring writer, purposeful practice is not merely writing every day but writing to enhance your skills. It entails examining sentence structure, experimenting with various storytelling approaches, and soliciting feedback. True mastery is gained by deliberate practice, which is the intentional pursuit of development.

Chapter 2: Developing the Right Mindset.

The journey to skill mastery is as much about mental attitude as physical effort. Your mentality determines how you approach learning, how you handle failures, and your capacity to persevere when things become difficult. A fixed attitude, which believes that intellect and talent are static, can only get you so far. A growth mindset, on the other hand, is the concept that talents and intellect can be improved through work and study, which may lead to endless opportunities.

The growth mindset: accepting challenges and failure.

A growth mindset is required to overcome the unavoidable hurdles associated with skill development. If you assume that your talents are fixed, each failure will seem like a personal setback. On the other hand, if you recognize that failure is a necessary part of the learning process, you may see each setback as a chance to improve. Challenges help us build resilience, perfect our methods, and discover new ways of doing things.

Consider the path of an Olympic athlete. They don't become champions overnight; they put in months, if not years, of tough training, dealing with failure after failure. However, each setback is seen as a stepping stone to future achievement. The same attitude is required to perfect every skill. Setbacks are unavoidable while learning to program, improving your public speaking talents, or honing your bargaining abilities. However, they are not a reflection of your potential; rather, they are a necessary step on the way to mastery.

Developing a development mindset also entails acknowledging that learning is a continuous process. You will never "arrive" at mastery in any profession; there is always space for growth. The most successful individuals constantly seek new challenges, broaden their knowledge, and push their limits. This thinking inspires both the desire to persevere and the resilience to overcome challenges.

How Your Financial Beliefs Shape Your Abilities.

Your attitudes about money and wealth may have a significant influence on your financial performance. If you think of money as something rare that you have to "earn" via hard work and sacrifice, your relationship with it may become filled with fear and limitations. On the other hand, if you think of money as a tool that comes effortlessly when you create value, you'll see possibilities rather than roadblocks.

Your financial perspective has a direct effect on how you approach skill development. People who have restrictive attitudes about money may be unwilling to invest in their education or take prudent risks. They may underestimate their abilities or hesitate to ask for what they are worth. In contrast, plenty of believers know that developing key skills can generate wealth for themselves and others.

A positive attitude toward money might encourage you to see skill development as an investment in your future. When you realize that the more value you provide, the better your financial prospects, you will pursue skill development with passion. Your financial success follows a logical progression of your dedication to personal development and learning.

Chapter 3: Practical Techniques for Skill Acquisition.

Mastering new skills can feel tricky, but with the right method, anyone can make the process more effective and fun. This chapter focuses on practical methods to learn faster and to retain knowledge better, with an emphasis on two core principles: focused practice and efficient use of tools and resources. By applying these techniques, you'll be able to accelerate your learning and become proficient in your chosen skills.

Accelerating learning through focused practice.

Focused practice is a deliberate, goal-oriented method of skill learning that centers on improving specific aspects of a skill through focused efforts. Unlike careless or irregular practice, focused practice needs diligence and purpose, urging you to push past your comfort zone and flourish faster.

1. Set clear, specific goals.
To make the most of focused practice, start by setting clear goals for what you want to achieve. Avoid vague goals like getting better at coding or learning to play the guitar. Instead, set measurable goals, like building a basic web page by the end of the week or? learning three new chords today.? These specific goals give your practice sessions direction, allowing you to track growth and make changes.

2. Break down skills into smaller components.
Complex skills can be stressful, but breaking them down into smaller, doable jobs allows for more effective learning. If you're learning a language, focus on words one day, grammar the next, and speech afterward. By separating parts of the skill, you can improve each aspect individually and combine them over time for a more complete understanding.

3. Use the 10,000-hour rule mindfully.
While the "10,000-hour rule" says it takes around 10,000 hours to

learn a skill, it's crucial to focus on the quality of your work rather than the quantity. Purposeful practice over shorter, focused times can often give faster results than unorganized, long lessons. Aim to practice in bursts of 30 to 45 minutes with breaks in between to keep energy and focus.

4. Embrace feedback and self-assessment.

Feedback is important to successful learning, as it gives insights into your work and areas needing growth. Seek feedback from teachers, peers, or online groups to improve your technique. Additionally, learn self-assessment by checking your work closely. Both types of input allow you to spot trends, fix mistakes, and move toward success.

Tools and resources to boost your learning efficiency.

With focused practice as a basis, the next step is to leverage the tools and resources available to support your journey. The right tools can simplify your learning process, provide order, and keep you inspired.

1. Digital learning platforms and apps.

The digital era has brought a wealth of learning tools and apps that make skill development more available than ever. Sites like Coursera, Udemy, and LinkedIn Learning offer classes in nearly any area, allowing you to learn from experts around the world. Apps like Duolingo, Memrise, and Blinkist provide specialized tools for language learning, memory, and summary information for quick consumption.

2. Habit-Tracking Apps and Productivity Tools.

To stay constant, try using habit-tracking apps like Habitica or Streaks to record your practice sessions and track growth. These apps let you set daily goals, track your habits over time, and enjoy milestones. Productivity tools like Trello, Notion, or Google Keep can help organize your learning materials, set goals, and make your work obvious.

3. Audio and video resources for multimodal learning.

Incorporating various media formats—audio, visual, and textual—helps strengthen learning by engaging different brain parts. Podcasts, YouTube lessons, and educational sites offer insights from experts and actual demos. Try learning from podcasts while traveling, watching video lessons during focused study time, and reading books or articles for greater understanding.

4. Practice platforms and simulators.

Interactive practice tools are essential for putting your information in real-world situations. For programming, websites like LeetCode, HackerRank, and GitHub allow you to practice code tasks, work on projects, and even interact with other learners. For language learning, sites like HelloTalk or Tandem provide chances to talk with native speakers, improving confidence and competence.

5. Online communities and mentoring.

Learning can feel private, but online groups offer friendship, support, and responsibility. Reddit, Quora, and Stack Overflow feature lively groups where people share insights, answer questions, and cooperate. Additionally, finding a coach in person or online can speed up your progress by providing personalized comments, advice, and support.

Summary.

Skill learning doesn't have to be overwhelming. By adding focused practice and leveraging helpful tools and resources, you can create a learning routine that is both enjoyable and effective. With clear goals, planned practice, and the right support systems, you'll be able to learn new skills faster and more easily, turning each new ability into a stepping stone toward personal and professional growth.

Chapter 4: Turning Skills into Opportunities.

Learning a skill is self-investment, but the journey continues. The next stage is to turn these abilities into revenue and opportunities. This chapter looks at how to monetize your knowledge via freelancing, coaching, and online courses, as well as how to create a personal brand that stands out and attracts customers, collaborators, and employers.

How to Make Money with Your Knowledge.

The gig economy and internet platforms have made it easier to commercialize abilities than ever before. Here are some prominent methods for converting your knowledge into cash streams:

1. Freelancing.

Freelancing is one of the quickest methods to monetize your expertise. Platforms such as Upwork, Fiverr, and Freelancer link qualified people with customers looking for specialized skills. Freelancing enables you to work on a project-by-project basis, providing you with more control over your workload, rates, and tasks. For example, if you are skilled in writing, graphic design, programming, or marketing, you may offer your services on freelancing sites and begin creating a customer base. Begin by taking on little jobs to create your portfolio and obtain favorable feedback, which will help you attract more customers over time.

2. Consulting and coaching.

Consulting or coaching may be a profitable choice for people with advanced knowledge or a specific area of skill. Consulting is giving customers advice and methods to help them handle particular challenges in their sector, such as enhancing corporate operations, developing digital marketing strategies, or optimizing product designs. Coaching is another approach that includes assisting people in achieving their objectives by honing their talents, whether in professional growth, fitness, language acquisition, or other personal areas. You may provide consultations via personal websites, LinkedIn, or specialist platforms such as Clarity.fm, which links professionals with customers seeking assistance.

3. Developing and selling online courses.

Creating an online course based on a skill you are proficient in enables you to reach a big audience while also generating passive revenue. Platforms like Udemy, Teachable, and Skillshare provide simple ways to build courses in several formats, including video lectures, interactive activities, and downloaded materials. Online classes are popular in almost every industry, including business, art, coding, fitness, and more. When developing a course, prioritize tackling particular issues and making the information actionable. For example, instead of taking a general marketing course, consider "Social Media Marketing for Small Businesses." This clarity attracts learners with unique interests and boosts course value.

4. Blogging, Vlogging, and Content Creation.

Creating content on sites such as YouTube, Medium, or a personal blog may also help you make money. Blogs and vlogs allow you to exhibit your knowledge while also monetizing it via adverts, sponsored articles, affiliate marketing, and brand collaborations. For example, if you're an expert in photography, a blog with advice, equipment suggestions, and lessons might garner a following and lead to income options. Building a social media following (Instagram, TikTok, or Twitter) around your content may also lead to company sponsorships or product collaborations in your specialty.

Creating a Personal Brand Around Your Expertise.

Creating a personal brand is vital for differentiating oneself and leaving a lasting impact in your area. A strong brand communicates who you are, what you do, and why to partner. Here's how to make a brand stand out:

1. Identify Your Niche and Value Proposition.

A specialty makes it simpler to stand out and build a dedicated following. Choose a particular area in your career where you excel.

Instead of calling yourself a "digital marketer," try "digital marketing for health and wellness businesses." Next, establish your value proposition: what unique value or insight do you offer to the table? This might be a unique strategy, technique, or style that distinguishes your work and provides prospective customers a reason to pick you above others.

2. Showcase Your Work Online.

Creating a portfolio website is a powerful method to highlight your abilities, previous projects, and customer testimonials. This might contain case studies, samples of prior work, or a blog with articles on your field of expertise. A well-curated online presence on LinkedIn or personal websites may boost your reputation and make it easier for others to locate you. Include an "About" section that describes your history and beliefs, a portfolio with specific samples of your work, and a contact form for possible customers or partners.

3. Create a content strategy.

Consistently publishing excellent information strengthens your expertise and keeps you prominent. Instead of being on every platform, choose one or two that your audience uses. If you're a designer, visual sites like Instagram and Dribbble are excellent for presenting your work. For authors, LinkedIn and Medium are fantastic options. Create material that provides insights or solutions that are relevant to your target audience's demands. For example, if you're a web developer, contribute ideas for increasing website speed or user experience. Consistent, high-quality content fosters trust and keeps your audience interested.

4. Engage your community.

Building a brand also requires active engagement with your target audience. Respond to comments, join online communities, and attend webinars or business events. Engaging with individuals in your area may lead to cooperation, mentoring, and partnerships that will help your brand. Authentic involvement, such as commenting on other people's postings or providing input on similar interests, helps you develop a network of meaningful contacts and solidify your expertise.

5. Use Testimonials and Case Studies.

Testimonials and case studies may be effective forms of social proof for developing a brand. Positive feedback from delighted customers not only demonstrates your capabilities but also fosters trust. Case studies are equally useful since they enable you to illustrate the effect of your effort. For example, if you helped a customer improve their website traffic by 50%, write a case study on the approach and outcomes. This may be included on your website or LinkedIn page to demonstrate your effectiveness.

Summary.

Turning talents into opportunities is a continuous process. There are several ways to make money from your skills, including freelancing, consulting, course building, and content generation. Building a personal brand strengthens these efforts by recruiting customers and colleagues who respect what you do. By using these tactics, you will not only generate revenue but also establish a reputation that will lead to future chances. Accept the challenge of monetizing your abilities and developing your brand. It's an effective approach to put your knowledge to work for you.

Conclusion: A Lifetime Journey of Skill and Wealth.

Learning is a continuous process, and in today's fast-changing world, it is more important than ever. The skills and information you gain are more than simply instruments for career progress; they are investments in personal growth, flexibility, and opportunity. In this book, we've looked at how to approach skill development efficiently and convert knowledge into money. Finally, consider why constant learning is essential and how adopting this approach may genuinely alter your life.

The importance of continuous learning

Today, technical and societal developments are reshaping sectors at an incredible rate. Skills that were previously in high demand may soon become outdated, and new possibilities may emerge in unexpected places. Anyone trying to stay relevant, build resilience, or produce wealth should embrace lifelong learning.

Continuous learning is more than just adding new abilities to your résumé. It is about developing a growth mindset that promotes curiosity, flexibility, and resilience. When you commit to learning on a regular basis, you improve your ability to negotiate change, seek new avenues, and create inventive solutions. Lifelong learners are more versatile, capable of pivoting in response to problems, and more receptive to new opportunities. This flexibility is crucial; it helps you to remain flexible and relevant as the world around you evolves.

More importantly, the learning process itself becomes extremely satisfying. Each new skill learned contributes to an increased feeling of self-confidence and competence. This confidence feeds additional exploration and ambition, propelling you to even higher heights. For individuals interested in wealth growth, this is a strong combination: learning broadens your talents, which in turn open doors to better income and more diverse options. By focusing on learning consistently, you may lay the groundwork for a foundation of knowledge and abilities that will support your financial and personal objectives indefinitely.

Final Thoughts on Changing Your Life with Ideas and Actions.

This book demonstrated that talents are more than simply competencies; they are roads to independence, advancement, and financial freedom. Acquiring abilities is the initial step, but it is how you use them that makes a lasting difference. Your talents are just as important as your actions with them. Whether you're turning your knowledge into a freelancing company, creating an online course, or connecting with people via your personal brand, converting abilities into opportunities needs a combination of perseverance, creativity, and smart thinking.

Ideas are what will power you on your trip. Every concept, whether it is a project vision or a new way of learning, has the potential to alter. By creating a mentality that values creativity, innovation, and continuous self-improvement, you may position yourself to see and grasp opportunities that others may miss. This approach enables you to translate information into action and action into effect.

Think of your abilities as the seeds of your future. You may nourish them via concentrated practice, and with purposeful action, you can see them blossom into accomplishments and possibilities. Each step forward increases momentum, allowing you to live a life marked by both personal satisfaction and financial resiliency.

Finally, remember that money, success, and satisfaction begin with ideas and are fulfilled via deliberate study and action. Building skills, goals, and habits is a continuous process. Accept it and let your dedication to study and progress constantly improve your life.

A short story

Several years ago, a young man named Kwame lived in a small town full of dreamers but with few resources. Like many others, Kwame had big dreams but felt trapped by his surroundings. He would spend hours watching successful people from a distance, wondering what secret they had that he didn't.

While wandering through the local market, one day, he came across an old man selling handmade items. This mentor taught him a profound truth: "Wealth is more than coins and bills. It's about the skills you learn and the ideas you bring to life." That moment planted a seed in Kwame's mind, and he decided to set out on a journey to discover his hidden potential.

Kwame started small. He learned a single skill: carving simple wooden figures. But he did not stop there. He studied marketing, customer service, and design, each of which contributed to his growing skill set. As his craft became a successful business, his ideas began to shape his and others' futures.

Years later, Kwame returned to that market, this time as a symbol of transformation. He was no longer just selling products; he was also teaching others how to develop their skills and turn their ideas into sources of wealth and purpose.

Kwame's story is not unique; it exemplifies a timeless truth. The journey to wealth begins with an idea, but it grows with the skills we choose to learn and refine.

As you finish this book, remember that your life's story is still unfolding. The techniques and insights you've gained will serve you well on your next journey. Like Kwame, you can transform every idea into an opportunity and every challenge into a stepping stone.

There is no end to your journey of skill and wealth—only new chapters to write. What will be your next idea?

About the Author: Gyabaah Gilbert Yeboah.

Gyabaah Gilbert Yeboah's journey is a living testament to the central message of his book, Money is an Idea: Effective Techniques for Acquiring Skills. Born with an insatiable curiosity and a knack for problem-solving, he transformed his early struggles into stepping stones toward success.

Growing up, Gilbert often found himself asking, "How do some people turn simple ideas into incredible achievements?" This question sparked his lifelong passion for understanding the intersection of creativity, skills, and wealth creation. With limited resources but boundless determination, he started turning his ideas into tangible results—learning new skills, building connections, and crafting opportunities where none existed.

From mastering the art of self-education to inspiring others to recognize the potential in their ideas, Gilbert has become a beacon for those who want to break free from conventional limits. Through his workshops, mentorship, and now his book, he shares the techniques that helped him—and countless others—transform ideas into prosperity.

When he's not writing or mentoring, Gilbert can be found exploring innovative ways to bridge knowledge and opportunity, always seeking to empower others with the belief that skills are the currency of the future. His story isn't just about success; it's about creating a roadmap for anyone ready to turn their ideas into wealth.

www.ingramcontent.com/pod-product-compliance
Lightning Source LLC
Chambersburg PA
CBHW030046230526
45472CB00005B/1707